SPIRITUAL GIFTS

ARE THEY STILL FOR

TODAY?

DARREN HIBBS

SPIRITUAL GIFTS

ARE THEY STILL FOR

TODAY?

DARREN HIBBS

10 Week Books

10WeekBooks.com

10 Week Books
10WeekBooks.com

For Emily

CONTENTS

ACKNOWLEDGEMENTS

I want to thank the Holy Spirit for His indwelling power—the power to love fully, live greatly and see clearly. I want to thank my beautiful wife, Sarah, for making room in our life for me to write, something I know the Lord has given me for this season. I would also like to thank my children for sharing their daddy's time with a computer screen for the sake of those who will read and be challenged to live for God. I pray these words will one day encourage you three also.

PREFACE

There has been a heightened interest in the debate over whether God still operates through the supernatural gifts of the Holy Spirit today. I have personally experienced God's move through His spiritual gifts, but I also understand people who are hesitant to believe in them. With anything as good and beneficial as God's spiritual gifts, there is excess and silliness that turns people off. I hope that this book will give you a new desire to seek God for His supernatural gifts as well as temper your understanding with some basic theological foundations of the gifts.

SPIRITUAL GIFTS

ARE THEY STILL FOR

TODAY?

1

INTRODUCTION TO SPIRITUAL GIFTS

In the past year, the issue of spiritual gifts has become a rather hot topic. Since the 1990's there has been a dramatic increase in the number of denominational and non-denominational churches and denominations embracing the operation of all the spiritual gifts today. Because of this, there has been significant push-back from some spheres in the Body of Christ that I believe deserves a response.

The thing that has concerned me is the tenor of the debate that has come up. It has not been one of debating points of scripture and their validity for today, but one that has been elevated to utmost importance. There are some who are currently trying to make a belief in the operation of all the spiritual gifts today into damnable offenses.

I have no problem with someone not believing in the gifts still in operation. I was that way, so I have great grace for that position, but to elevate an issue like spiritual gifts to the same plane as the gospel itself bothers me deeply. Nowhere in scripture was any writer ever concerned with heresy that did not have to do with turning people away from the gospel of truth. We are commanded to oppose people who distort the truth of Jesus' deity, sacrifice and atonement. Spiritual gifts are a secondary matter of theology that has been elevated to unbiblical levels. This book is a fresh look at the spiritual gifts today.

MY STORY

I should start by stating that I have personally experienced the grace of God through spiritual gifts, especially prophecy. I was raised as a cessationist in a Baptist church. I am eternally grateful for the 99% of what I was taught at that church as being biblically orthodox and useful. It is the 1% that was cessationism that I have come to reject. When I was still young I began questioning the truth behind many of the claims I heard about the gifts.

Instead of just taking my pastor and other teachers at their word, I began to study the Word of God for myself. I came to believe that the Bible said that spiritual gifts were definitely still for today. I could find no evidence in scripture for cessation of any of the gifts. At the same time I started asking God in prayer to reveal to me if He truly still did the stuff He did in the Bible. At that time I had a few experiences that solidified my belief He did in fact still do "the stuff" He did in scripture.

EXPERIENTIAL THEOLOGY

Some people want to preach to you that your theology cannot be based on experience, but that is simply not possible. I do not claim to have come to my conclusions simply out of my study of scripture alone. I am not smart enough to do that and neither is anyone else on planet earth. Peter had all of the Old Testament at his disposal to understand that Jesus was the "Messiah, the Son of God," but Jesus told him he came to that conclusion because "My Father has revealed this to you" (Matthew 16:13-19).

Our experience with the Spirit of Truth (the Holy Spirit) is indelibly bound to our understanding of theology. The problem is not when our experience informs our theology, but when our experience causes us to get it wrong. Experience by itself is neither good nor bad. It is like the internet. It can be used for great good or horrible wickedness. Experience is good when it leads us to proper conclusions and bad when it leads us down the wrong path. All of our understandings are tied to our experience, so we must not throw out experience, but rather evaluate the relevance of our experience to any theological position.

2

DID THE SPIRITUAL GIFTS CEASE?

The Questions We Must Answer:

1. Does scripture say some gifts ceased?
2. How did we get this idea?
3. Where did modern cessationism originate?

Before we begin, let's look at the pertinent passages of scripture:

> *3For by the grace given me I say to every one of you: Do not think of yourself more highly than you ought, but rather think of yourself with sober judgment, in accordance with the faith God has distributed to each of you. 4For just as each of us has one body with many members, and these members do not all have the same function, 5so in Christ we, though many, form one body, and each member belongs to all the*

others. ⁶We have different gifts, according to the grace given to each of us. If your gift is prophesying, then prophesy in accordance with your faith; ⁷if it is serving, then serve; if it is teaching, then teach; ⁸if it is to encourage, then give encouragement; if it is giving, then give generously; if it is to lead, do it diligently; if it is to show mercy, do it cheerfully.

Romans 12:3-8

⁷Now to each one the manifestation of the Spirit is given for the common good. ⁸To one there is given through the Spirit a message of wisdom, to another a message of knowledge by means of the same Spirit, ⁹to another faith by the same Spirit, to another gifts of healing by that one Spirit, ¹⁰to another miraculous powers, to another prophecy, to another distinguishing between spirits, to another speaking in different kinds of tongues, and to still another the interpretation of tongues. ¹¹All these are the work of one and the same Spirit, and he distributes them to each one, just as he determines.

1 Corinthians 12:7-11

¹¹So Christ himself gave the apostles, the prophets, the evangelists, the pastors and teachers, ¹²to equip his people for works of service, so that the body of Christ may be built up ¹³until we all reach unity in the faith and in the knowledge of the Son of God and become mature, at-

taining to the whole measure of the fullness of Christ.

Ephesians 4:11-13

1. CESSATIONISM: DID THE GIFTS CEASE?

Cessationism is the belief that some of the spiritual gifts listed in scripture are no longer in operation today. I do not believe this is an accurate theological perspective for many reasons. The first and most obvious reason is that the list of gifts many people believe have ceased are biblically arbitrary.

Most cessationists would claim that apostles and prophets no longer exist as well as any miraculous gifts associated with them such as prophecy, healing, miracles, tongues, words of wisdom and supernatural knowledge. They believe that offices like pastors, teachers and evangelists are still in operation as well as gifts like helps, administration, discernment and service to name a few.

The problem with claiming some gifts have ceased and others have not, as well as the answer to our first question, is that there are absolutely no Bible verses that explicitly say any of these gifts that are listed have ceased. That means that any list of gifts that have ceased must be derived from some interpretation of scripture. There are verses that claim one day prophecy will cease, but they are all in reference to the millennial kingdom or eternity, depending on your view of the end times. (Zechariah 12-13 and 1 Corinthians 13)

Deriving a theological point is not a bad practice in and of itself. It is part of any study in systematic theology. Scripture does not always explicitly say something, but it may allude to a truth over and over throughout. We must be careful, however, when we derive a theological perspective that stands in direct contradiction to clearly stated scriptural passages. Such is the case with spiritual gifts.

2. HOW DID WE GET THIS IDEA?

To overcome the very explicit nature of the passages listed above, we should have an overwhelming body of proof in scripture that would give us license to believe the gifts had ceased. We do not. What cessationists point to as their rationale is the motive behind scripture. They draw conjecture upon the plans and purposes of scripture itself and then draw conclusions based upon that.

As an example, many cessationists would say that the scripture's purpose is to illuminate the message of God. Since we (as Protestant Evangelicals, to be exact) believe that the canon of scripture is closed, then we have the fully revealed work of God with no need of anything else. As the thinking goes, anything that God used to create the closed canon of scripture would now be unnecessary, such as prophecy, healing, tongues and miracles. Apostles and prophets would also cease since they were the framers of scripture. These were temporary gifts, as cessationists would say, because they were only given to fulfill the purpose of scripture. Now that we have the complete Bible, we have no more need of them so God has discontinued His giving of them.

Unfortunately, this simply is not true. This theology is based on a preconceived notion, however noble, that we have the license to determine theology based on our ideas about God's motives. Reading into scripture God's motives that are not explicit is a very dangerous hermeneutical approach that has led to this incorrect teaching. The Bible does say that certain supernatural gifts were useful for affirming God's anointing of His ministers like apostles and prophets, but it does not say that their only purpose was to fulfill the fully re-vealed canon of scripture. In fact, that idea doesn't ex-ist in scripture—it is a theological leap that simply isn't there.

Scripture itself does not speak to scripture ending. The closing of the canon of scripture was not a decision handed down by the apostles in scripture, but a gener-ally accepted list of books that were useful to the early church—books they felt should be added to the list of Old Testament books as foundational to the revelation of God. As orthodox Christians, we believe that God guided the hands of the early church to accept those books that were God-breathed and to reject those that weren't. The idea that the canon is closed is itself a testimony to the idea that God's supernatural power and intervention lived on long past the apostles listed in the New Testament.

To the contrary of what cessationists believe, scripture makes it clear that all the gifts He has given to His people are available until the day He returns. Paul tells us to "eagerly desire spiritual gifts, especially that you may prophesy." (1 Corinthians 14:1). That is simply too clear a command to will away because of theological conjecture.

3. WHERE DID (MODERN) CESSATIONISM ORIGINATE?

Modern cessationism has its roots in the Reformation. The idea of "Sola Scriptura," or only scripture, was one of the mantras of the Reformation. The idea was in reaction to the Catholic belief that God's revelation did not end with the closing of the canon of scripture. Catholics believe that God has and still does use the Pope to hand out new revelation (forgive me, my Catholic brethren if I am painting with too large a brush of generalities for the sake of time). In response to what the Reformers considered Catholic heresies, this was one of the primary distinctions made during the Reformation. They stated in contrast to the Catholics that no new revelation was being given. It led them to conjecture that God had ceased the super-natural or "sign gifts" when He was done with scripture.

Just to be clear, I agree with the Reformers, that God has closed the canon of scripture and no new biblical revelation is being laid out anymore. That, however, is not a strictly biblical belief, which I have already pointed out.

This idea that miracles had ceased was never a commonly accepted idea within Protestantism until the beginning of the 20th Century. We have far too many stories of supernatural events in the lives and journals of spiritual leaders since the Protestant Reformation to believe so. What changed was the reaction to something that would eventually change the face of the worldwide church.

AZUSA

The Azusa Street revival in the Los Angeles area in the early years of the 20th century was a dynamic and strange new move in American Christianity. It was marked by a heavy emphasis on speaking in tongues. This was the move of God that sparked the Pentecostal movement, most prominently recognized by Pentecostal and Assembly of God churches.

The actions of many within the revival and ensuing movement were repugnant to members of the media and others in Los Angeles, where they received mixed reviews. This began a firestorm of back and forth that we can still see today. A common Pentecostal idea developed that if you hadn't received tongues, you weren't filled with the Holy Spirit. The response to that was that the gifts must certainly not be in existence today because God wouldn't approve of such foolishness.

We will deal with this idea further chapter seven about tongues.

So modern cessationism has its roots in the Reformation, but it was an idea solidified after the Azusa Street revivals. Cessationism is a theological perspective that does not have a solid biblical basis and is formed upon extra-biblical assumptions and reactions that are incorrect. The Bible is very clear that all the spiritual gifts given in the New Testament are to be understood as still in operation today.

That leads us to our next topic that cessationists point to regularly.

3

ARE THERE COUNTERFEIT GIFTS?

One main point that many cessationists often use to justify their belief is that of the existence of counterfeit spiritual gifts. Let's pose two questions:

1. Do counterfeit spiritual gifts exist?
2. If so, what should be done about them?

COUNTERFEIT GIFTS

The answer should depend on whether you believe that God still gives all the spiritual gifts today or not. If God does not still give out all the spiritual gifts, as cessationists would argue, then counterfeit gifts cannot exist.

Because we are speaking in metaphor, we will analyze according to that metaphor. Only good currency is ever counterfeited. Money that cannot truly be used is not worthy of counterfeit. Would anyone counterfeit Monopoly money? Of course not, because you cannot buy anything with it in the first place. Counterfeit only has value because it is mimicking something real. That would make the idea of counterfeit spiritual gifts absurd if they do not exist anymore. I will stop here so we do not venture off into hyperbole.

We cannot take the metaphor of counterfeit gifts too far, but at this level it is a valid argument. We have an enemy who is "hell" bent upon destruction, devouring and deception. He can, will and does masquerade as an "angel of light." If we believe that God still grants spiritual gifts, we would be foolish to be unaware of such a scheme of the devil, as Paul would say.

> *13 For such people are false apostles, deceitful workers, masquerading as apostles of Christ. 14 And no wonder, for Satan himself masquerades as an angel of light. 15 It is not surprising, then, if his servants also masquerade as servants of righteousness. Their end will be what their actions deserve.*
>
> *2 Corinthians 11:13-15*

HOW DO WE KNOW?

Examples of counterfeit gifts can be found throughout the Bible. The great thing about them is they are (as best I can remember) always contrasted by more powerful demonstrations of true gifts. Take Moses and the magicians of Egypt for example (Exodus 7:22). The magicians were able to reproduce the first few miraculous signs that Moses and Aaron performed, but even then they were inferior. When Aaron threw his staff down and it became a snake, it went and ate the staffs the magicians had done the same thing with. Very quickly the Egyptian magicians were not able to reproduce what Moses and Aaron could do by the will of God.

Anything counterfeit can only be passed off as real by someone unskilled to tell the difference. A well-trained checker at a grocery store knows the procedures to follow to determine whether money is real or fake. The same can be said of real and counterfeit miracles, signs, wonders and prophecies.

Moses instructed the people in this way about counterfeiters (false prophets):

> *1If a prophet, or one who foretells by dreams, appears among you and announces to you a sign or wonder, 2and if the sign or wonder spoken of takes place, and the prophet says, "Let us follow other gods" (gods you have not known) "and let us worship them," 3you must not listen to the words of that prophet or dreamer. The Lord your God is testing you to find out whether you love him with all your heart and with all your soul. 4It is the Lord your God you*

must follow, and him you must revere. Keep his commands and obey him; serve him and hold fast to him. ⁵That prophet or dreamer must be put to death for inciting rebellion against the Lord your God, who brought you out of Egypt and redeemed you from the land of slavery. That prophet or dreamer tried to turn you from the way the Lord your God commanded you to follow. You must purge the evil from among you.

Deuteronomy 13:1-5

The idea here is that someone would come along who could really perform a sign or a wonder just like Moses and Aaron had done. Signs are used to give credibility to a prophet's message. If a prophet tells you to go move to another town, then how are you to know whether or not his message is truly from God? Now if that prophet tells you that you need to move to another town and as a confirming sign there will be an earthquake on such a date, I would take his word more seriously. That is the point of a sign—it lends credibility to a prophet. But the true litmus test for a prophet was not whether or not his sign came to pass, but whether his intentions were to follow another god, or the one true God.

Moses told the people that God would allow such a thing as a test, to see whether they truly loved Him, or just wanted a cool, easy fix for a problem. The issue at hand is judging what makes a false prophet, or someone performing counterfeit signs and gifts.

WHAT DO WE DO WITH COUNTERFEITERS?

Extreme positions are easy to run to. They are black and white and they make sense to our finite minds. "God does this, but not that," is an easy position to hold, but often times the truth is more nuanced than that. The truth, about a great many things, sounds like this: "God does this most of the time, doesn't do this much, and I'm not sure why He did this."

Calling people "false prophets" and counterfeits, charlatans, etc. Is an easy extreme to run to, but we as God's people must be more careful than that. Remember, our litmus test was whether or not that false prophet was leading people to another God. Jesus proclaimed the same test in Matthew 24:24 as does Paul in Galatians 1:8-9 and 2 Corinthians 11:4.

Often times people are labeled as false prophets, counterfeits and charlatans simply because their prophesies turn out to be incorrect. According to scripture, that does not make them "false prophets" or counterfeits. It makes them wrong. To be a counterfeit or a false prophet, one must be trying to lead others away from Jesus. Anyone who prophesies incorrectly or anything else in the name of Jesus is not to be labeled counterfeit. Jesus told the disciples this regarding such things:

49"Master," said John, "we saw someone driving out demons in your name and we tried to stop him, because he is not one of us."

50"Do not stop him, "Jesus said, "for whoever is not against you is for you."

Luke 9:49-50

Great harm has been done to other members of the body of Christ because the test for counterfeit has been inappropriately applied. If someone who loves and serves Jesus incorrectly or inappropriately uses spiritual gifts, that doesn't make them false or counterfeit, it simply makes them wrong. To point out that wrong and steer them back in the right direction in love is the honor and dignity we possess as fellow believers. To consider those who truly follow Jesus as counterfeit for being wrong is unbiblical.

Some cessationists still do this because of a misunderstanding of another passage in Deuteronomy.

17The Lord said to me: "What they say is good. 18I will raise up for them a prophet like you from among their fellow Israelites, and I will put my words in his mouth. He will tell them everything I command him. 19I myself will call to account anyone who does not listen to my words that the prophet speaks in my name. 20But a prophet who presumes to speak in my name anything I have not commanded, or a prophet who speaks in the name of other gods, is to be put to death."

Deuteronomy 18:17-20

We understand from this context that this is mostly about Jesus being the prophet like Moses, but verse 20 trips people up sometimes. "A prophet who presumes to speak in my name anything I have not commanded" does not mean someone who is simply wrong, but someone who is again trying to lead people away from God. I've never met anyone today willing to cast that first stone for someone being wrong. In fact, there is only one biblical reference to this command ever being carried out, and that was with Balaam.

Balaam attempted to falsely prophesy against Israel, but several times could not. Eventually it was he who instructed the King of Moab to lead the children of Israel astray by fornication with their young women. Joshua killed Balaam later when he found him for the treachery of trying to turn God's people away from Him.

Our reaction must be different today, however. Almost all New Testament Christians would agree that putting someone to death for being a false prophet is not our place anymore. Christianity is not a unified theocratic government, but an interconnected band of people stitched together by the bonds of love for God. We do not possess the right to execute as sovereign

Israel did to whom Moses was giving this command. Instead, we must oppose and call out false prophets today. We must warn others of them. Men like Jim Jones and David Koresh who were actual false prophets and counterfeits—men for one reason or another who lead people away to Jesus and to themselves or some other false god or religion—they are the ones we must oppose and give our energies to confront.

To conclude for today, we can answer our two questions: 1) counterfeit gifts do exist today, because God is still giving all His gifts and we have an enemy who is always deceiving and 2)If we find someone who is truly false (and not just wrong), the we must oppose them and educate people around us of their motives to lead them away from Jesus.

4

SEEKING SPIRITUAL GIFTS

My "birth" into believing in the contemporary operation of all the spiritual gifts began in 1 Corinthians 14.
Because of that, I have tried to apply to my life Paul's
command in verse one. "Follow the way of love and
eagerly desire gifts of the Spirit, especially prophecy."

I figured out very early on that if God was still doing
these supernatural things like He did in the Bible, it
would be foolish for me not to ask for them. I began
asking God for them every day, and especially for
prophecy, for five years. During those five years, I
never experienced anything I would consider prophetic. That all changed when I went on a mission trip
to Guatemala in 2000. I have written about those experiences in a forthcoming book called A Diary of
Dreams and Visions, due out in late November 2013.

HE STARTED SPEAKING

Once the Lord started speaking to me prophetically, it radically transformed my life. Believing in the gifts of the Holy Spirit were no longer an academic pursuit for me, but an experiential one. Before I first experienced them personally, I was more apt to argue with people about why they were wrong for not believing in them, something I had only recently changed my own mind about. After I began experiencing them, I realized they were a grace of God far beyond my control. It immediately mellowed my desire to "bump heads" with people who thought differently.

The reason was because I now understood that people will not experience God in their lives through spiritual gifts, any spiritual gifts, unless their experiences are birthed in prayer. Far too many people today live content to believe that God still speaks, heals, performs miracles, etc., but mainly only through other people. Few people (albeit a rapidly growing number) have experienced the gifts for themselves, simply because they have not asked.

IT TOOK TIME

I am not trying to cast a shadow of shame on believers for not asking. I completely understand why people do not ask. Maybe they started asking, but gave up after a while because the Lord hadn't spoken to them. I have met too many people to count who have this very experience. While it is difficult and painful, I believe Jesus spoke about this through a parable in Luke 18.

1Then Jesus told his disciples a parable to show them that they should always pray and not give up. 2He said: "In a certain town there was a judge who neither feared God nor cared what people thought. 3And there was a widow in that town who kept coming to him with the plea, 'Grant me justice against my adversary.'

> 4"For some time he refused. But finally he said to himself, 'Even though I don't fear God or care what people think, 5yet because this widow keeps bothering me, I will see that she gets justice, so that she won't eventually come and attack me!' "
>
> 6And the Lord said, "Listen to what the unjust judge says. 7And will not God bring about justice for his chosen ones, who cry out to him day and night? Will he keep putting them off? 8I tell you, he will see that they get justice, and quickly. However, when the Son of Man comes, will he find faith on the earth?"
>
> Luke 18:1-8

PATIENCE

We must continue to pray for things, even if we don't get an answer right away. I prayed for five years without God ever answering me prophetically, but the long wait was worth the result. Even today I struggle to remember to ask God on a regular basis, so reading back over 1 Corinthians 14 recharges my drive to hear from God.

I think it is helpful to think about the spiritual gifts somewhat philosophically. If God exists and He is good, it only makes sense to seek after the very things He commanded us to do that are for our benefit and the benefit of the church. Spiritual gifts are not something we can believe in. They must be something we reject or something we earnestly seek after and encounter; there is no in-between.

My encouragement is that if you believe God still speaks, heals, raises the dead and performs miracles, then do not waste an opportunity to pray for a sick person. Do not forget to ask God His thoughts and opinions as often as you can. When you meet a dead person, pray for them to be raised. When you need a miracle, ask God for it.

MAKE A PLAN

That all seems very simple, but in my opinion most people who consider themselves Charismatic or Pentecostal do not actually ask God to experience the gifts for themselves. The main reason they do not is simply because they forget to ask. It's the same reason I don't ask and the same reason you don't take everything you need to the Lord in prayer.

The greatest way to fulfill Paul's command in 1 Corinthians 14:1 is to make a plan to pray. Don't just hope that prayer will happen throughout your day. If you do that, more than likely it won't happen much. If you make a plan, you may fall short of your plan, but you will pray, and remember to pray, far more than you would otherwise.

And the prayers God answers are always the ones we pray, not the ones we don't.

5

IS PROPHECY ONLY FOR
SCRIPTURE?

When I was a devout cessationist, I believed that prophecy was a pastor who taught well, I suppose as opposed to most "normal" pastors. I never thought that through very much, but it actually seems like a dig against pastors more than a valid explanation of what modern prophecy is. Who would want to consider their preaching NOT prophetic if that is the definition?

Two of the prevailing arguments against modern prophecy is that it 1) must always be correct and 2) it was only used to author scripture. The first argument is definitely a biblical idea, but lacks a common sense reading of the passages it comes from. The idea that God only used prophets and prophecy to author scripture is simply not a biblical concept.

The first issue comes from a passage in Deuteronomy when Moses is speaking about prophets. Let's read it:

14The nations you will dispossess listen to those who practice sorcery or divination. But as for you, the Lord your God has not permitted you to do so. 15The Lord your God will raise up for you a prophet like me from among you, from your fellow Israelites. You must listen to him. 16For this is what you asked of the Lord your God at Horeb on the day of the assembly when you said, "Let us not hear the voice of the Lord our God nor see this great fire anymore, or we will die."

17The Lord said to me: "What they say is good. 18I will raise up for them a prophet like you from among their fellow Israelites, and I will put my words in his mouth. He will tell them everything I command him. 19I myself will call to account anyone who does not listen to my words that the prophet speaks in my name. 20But a prophet who presumes to speak in my name anything I have not commanded, or a prophet who speaks in the name of other gods, is to be put to death."

> 21You may say to yourselves, "How can we know when a message has not been spoken by the Lord?" 22If what a prophet proclaims in the name of the Lord does not take place or come true, that is a message the Lord has not spoken.

That prophet has spoken presumptuously, so do not be alarmed.

Deuteronomy 18:14-22

We must first agree that this passage is mostly speaking about Jesus. The "prophet like me" is speaking about the Messiah to come. The penalty for not listening to Him would be God Himself calling to account anyone who does not listen to Him (at the judgment seat).

We must understand that verse 20 is mostly in context to this coming prophet. The problem with applying this passage to just about any prophet, biblical or not, becomes very difficult when we consider the timing of some prophecies. If we must put to death prophets whose prophecies do not come true, then Isaiah, Daniel, Ezekiel, Zechariah, John, etc. should all have been put to death. They all prophesied about things that did not come to pass in their lifetimes. Were they speaking presumptuously? Certainly not!

Jeremiah prophesied about the coming destruction of Jerusalem. He was labeled a false prophet by his peers because his prophesies did not come to pass immediately. This was the case with most of the prophets. They were persecuted or martyred for their words from God, presumably under the guise of obeying Deuteronomy 18, but Jesus Himself condemns the Pharisees for this (Matthew 23:30-31). Even though it seemed they were obeying God, they were completely wrong. So there must be some context we can apply to Deuteronomy 18 to understand how to judge false prophets from true ones.

That context is supplied earlier in Deuteronomy, in chapter 13:

> *¹If a prophet, or one who foretells by dreams, appears among you and announces to you a sign or wonder, ²and if the sign or wonder spoken of takes place, and the prophet says, "Let us follow other gods" (gods you have not known) "and let us worship them," ³you must not listen to the words of that prophet or dreamer. The Lord your God is testing you to find out whether you love him with all your heart and with all your soul. ⁴It is the Lord your God you must follow, and him you must revere. Keep his commands and obey him; serve him and hold fast to him. ⁵That prophet or dreamer must be put to death for inciting rebellion against the Lord your God, who brought you out of Egypt and redeemed you from the land of slavery. That prophet or dreamer tried to turn you from the way the Lord your God commanded you to follow. You must purge the evil from among you.*
>
> *Deuteronomy 13:1-5*

The true test for a false prophet is not whether their prophecies come true, but who their prophecies point to. If their prophecies and signs come true, but they want us to follow other gods, they are false prophets.

There are countless stories in scripture of the true prophets being persecuted and the false prophets being rewarded because of the sinful hearts of the people around them. God calls us to repentance, humility, holiness and love. False prophets will call us to license, greed, depravity and lust. One points to the god of this world and the other points to the God of eternity. Our judgments should be based on that, not only on whether the prophecies come true.

If someone prophesies that God will return on some date in the near future, as many have, and it doesn't happen, it is fairly easy to make judgment calls about that. It does not take great scriptural insight to label that person wrong. Common sense would direct people to stop listening to such a person (although many lack that common sense). I still would withhold the label "false" unless their prophecies of the end were to point people to other gods. If they preach Jesus and Jesus alone, I would not call them a "false prophet." A better term might be a "wrong prophet" or simply just not a prophet at all. Like Moses said, we need not fear them.

The fact that there were schools for prophets in Samuel's day is proof that prophets don't just get born with an unbroken track record of being right. Like any other gift or discipline, we must grow in it. Take Paul's command here;

> *27If anyone speaks in a tongue, two—or at the most three—should speak, one at a time, and someone must interpret. 28If there is no interpreter, the speaker should keep quiet in the church and speak to himself and to God.*
>
> *1 Corinthians 14:27-28*

First, there is considerable risk in speaking in a tongue in church. How do you know if there is an interpreter for a tongue unless you speak it forth? Someone has to test it out first. Paul is instructing the Corinthians not to keep on babbling if there is no interpreter, but someone has to step out and test the waters in this case. In the same way, in verse 29 Paul commands the church to weigh any prophecy with discernment. He says nothing about killing someone deemed not to have a true word.

The church must be a safe place to risk being wrong. That doesn't mean we give a platform to someone who is habitually wrong, but no one can learn to prophesy, or anything else for that matter, unless we make space to grow. That means getting it wrong and getting it right. Paul understood human nature enough to know that during any service, tongues should be limited to three people at most. Why? Because it doesn't take long for human nature to kick in and start copying, etc., even if God is truly moving, but neither did Paul limit it to "none."

The second objection to modern prophets is that they were only given to reveal scripture. This is a baseless argument. There were many prophets in scripture whose words are not recorded in the Bible. Whole "companies" in fact (1 Samuel 10:5-6; 19:19-24, 2 Kings 9:1-3 just to name three). The qualifying factor for authoring scripture is not prophecy. Look at the various writers of scripture. Some were prophets (Daniel). Some were apostles (Matthew). Some were neither (Luke). Other books have unknown authors (Hebrews). The fact is that there is no common thread among authors of scripture except that God chose them for their special task.

It has been by the decision of the early church, not by scriptural mandate, to close the Canon of Scripture. We believe in the wisdom of those who have gone before us that they were led to include the books of the Bible that are direct revelations from God and reject those that weren't. The very belief that the Canon is closed requires us to believe in the continuation of God's supernatural leading upon the church and His people. Without it, our faith is on shaky soil because our holy text would be suspect. It was just as direct a move of God to close the canon as it was to write it.

We cannot conclude, therefore, that prophets were only for the revelation of scripture. They are a necessary, and as we'll discuss later, primary role needed in the church then and today. Prophets and prophecy has not changed from the earliest prophets in scripture until now. Today we are all subservient to the revealed and closed Canon of Scripture as our foundation of judgment. A false prophet today is not one who prophesies, or even prophesies wrong, but one who prophesies against the written Word of God.

6

ARE THERE APOSTLES AND PROPHETS TODAY?

The follow on to the previous chapter about prophets is the question of whether or not there are still apostles today. I will continue the discussion about prophets here as they are very nearly related in scripture and many peoples' minds today.

First, "apostle" is a loaded word for Christians. Many believers immediately think of the twelve apostles Jesus appointed (with Matthias instead of Judas), and rightly so. They are referred to as the "apostles of the Lamb." They were a special set of apostles in the same way that Jacob's twelve sons were specially set apart for God's purposes. We see this clearly represented in the Lord's plans for the eternal Jerusalem in Revelation 21:9-27. This special status does not mean that they were never to be other apostles.

DEFINITIONS

The word apostle literally means "one sent out." Like a police officer stopping traffic, their upheld hand halts traffic not because of their own power over a car, but because of the authority that stands behind them. Disobey one police officer's stop sign and you must contend with an entire enforcement and legal system supporting him. The same is true with an apostle, they are ones sent out with the authority of the kingdom of heaven. That means that apostleship carries a mandate and authority.

Just like the other offices and spiritual gifts Paul lists in scripture, there are no direct definitions for apostleship, but Paul does give us some helpful hints.

One common reason people reject the idea of modern-day apostles is because they say scripture necessitates a direct encounter with Jesus. In 1 Corinthians 9:1 Paul alludes to his visitation from the resurrected Jesus as proof of his apostleship. This is a very interesting argument Paul makes, and it actually makes the case against most cessationists' viewpoint. If he had not said this, it could be very easy to discern from scripture that the only apostles were the twelve chosen by Jesus. But as it is, Paul never physically met the risen Jesus, but only in a vision. That opens the doors to apostles continuing if spiritual appearance, and not physical only, is a test for apostleship. It cannot be said biblically that it cannot happen to others today as it did to Paul.

We cannot draw a distinction between Paul's apostleship and a potential apostle today. Paul's visitation from Jesus would have been completely subjective. If we take him to mean that he met Jesus on the road to Damascus, even then we see that those with him did not experience what he did. So if Paul could meet Jesus in such a way, why would anyone today be prevented from doing so? Seeing Jesus like Paul would depend on someone's word about a subjective experience then, but Paul doesn't stop with that.

DRAWING SOME CLARITY

In 2 Corinthians 12:12 he is a little more clear, "I persevered in demonstrating among you the marks of a true apostle, including signs, wonders and miracles."

Notice that Paul doesn't limit the marks of true apostleship to signs, wonders and miracles. They are not the definitive sign of apostleship, but only evidence of it. Workers of miracles, one of the gifts God gives for instance, may perform miracles and not necessarily be apostles. A sign of true apostleship is the evidence of miracles, signs and wonders, but that would still be inconclusive.

That leaves us with a much more subjective reality than many would like. In our effort to create a clean-fit, cut-and-dry requirement for an apostle, we are still left with only partial evidence and discernment of subjective experiences. And that is exactly what Paul dealt with during his day as well.

> *Even though I may not be an apostle to others, surely I am to you! For you are the seal of my apostleship in the Lord.*
>
> *1 Corinthians 9:2*

WHAT MAKES AN APOSTLE?

This brings us to the truly discernible seal of an apostle: their fruit. Paul is not making a case of his apostleship before others who do not know him, but to the Corinthians who know him well. They saw his miracles. They heard his teaching. They saw the growth of the church while Paul was there. Even if no one else could verify to the Corinthians that Paul was an apostle, he makes the case that they should be sure of it themselves.

Going back to our discussion previously, there is no biblical evidence that apostles, prophets, miracles or any other gifts have ceased. Since Paul has laid out the case for what makes him an apostle, we can see no clear distinction between what made him one then and what would make an apostle today.

One passage people sometimes use to question modern apostles today is Paul's statement in 1 Corinthians 15:

> *3For what I received I passed on to you as of first importance : that Christ died for our sins according to the Scriptures, 4that he was buried, that he was raised on the third day according to the Scriptures, 5and that he appeared to Cephas, and then to the Twelve. 6After that, he appeared to more than five hundred of the brothers and sisters at the same time, most of whom are still living, though some have fallen asleep. 7Then he appeared to James, then to all the apostles, 8and last of all he appeared to me also, as to one abnormally born.*
>
> *9For I am the least of the apostles and do not even deserve to be called an apostle, because I persecuted the church of God. 10But by the grace of God I am what I am, and his grace to me was not without effect. No, I worked harder than all of them—yet not I, but the grace of God that was with me. 11Whether, then, it is I or they, this is what we preach, and this is what you believed.*
>
> *1 Corinthians 15:3-11*

NO MORE?

The argument is that Paul says he is the "last" of the apostles. Paul is not necessarily claiming to be the last apostle, but the last in the line he is referencing. I will admit that it could be argued that he is saying he was in fact the last, but that would seem arbitrary, especially given the rest of 1 Corinthians. Paul is trying to make the case here not that he was the last of the apostles, but the least.

He is speaking from a place of humility, knowing that he did not have the same experience as the rest of those considered apostles, especially the apostles of the lamb, but that he still was because of God's grace and ordination. To conclude that Paul was exerting himself the last apostle from this passage would be to deny his intention to call himself the least.

I will say that many Christians have a healthy skepticism of self-professed apostles, as they should. A healthy skepticism of anyone who calls themselves and apostle, prophet, or for that matter, teacher, does us some good. A little proof goes a long way, and we should not take anyone's word for such things.

We would do well to wield such terms as apostle and prophet delicately and with discernment. They carry the connotation of authority, an authority we should be careful to take up for ourselves. To be clear, scripture makes no claim that apostles or prophets have ceased, but it does warn that walking in such a position should be understood properly.

THE LIFESTYLE OF AN APOSTLE

Paul tells us just how carefully we should treat that term:

> *⁹For it seems to me that God has put us apostles on display at the end of the procession, like those condemned to die in the arena. We have been made a spectacle to the whole universe, to angels as well as to human beings. ¹⁰We are fools for Christ, but you are so wise in Christ! We are weak, but you are strong! You are honored, we are dishonored! ¹¹To this very hour we go hungry and thirsty, we are in rags, we are brutally treated, we are homeless. ¹²We work hard with our own hands. When we are cursed, we bless; when we are persecuted, we endure it; ¹³when we are slandered, we answer kindly. We have become the scum of the earth, the garbage of the world—right up to this moment.*
>
> *1 Corinthians 4:9-13*

Many that I have personally seen claim to be apostles do not exhibit this kind of lifestyle at all. They require obedience, honor and money to support them as God's chosen people. That is a big red flag to me. I have, however, witnessed a few who claim apostleship who live like this passage. I have the greatest confidence that they truly are apostles when I see this kind of laying down of their lives for others.

That is probably the greatest mark and test of an apostle: do they lead others with authority to lay down their lives for the sake of Jesus, or to take it up for their own victory?

7

DOES HOLY SPIRIT BAPTISM
REQUIRE TONGUES?

Tongues.

You probably read that word and had a reaction. Good or bad, I'm 99% sure it caused a reaction in you. There is almost no subject in the Christian vernacular as polarizing as tongues. Does God still give them? Are they required as evidence of Holy Spirit baptism? Does it happen all at once or as two separate encounters?

To start with, I affirm that the Lord still gives and uses the gift of tongues today like He did in scripture. I believe there are two primary roles tongues fulfill. They are 1) public usage and 2) private prayer.

IN PUBLIC

The public display of tongues is like that seen in Acts 2 on the day of Pentecost. Acts does not actually give us a good description as to the mechanics of how it worked on that day, only that it did. Did the disciples think they were speaking in their own language and everyone else was actually receiving the "gift of ears," or were they babbling on in an unintelligible language to themselves? As is biblically the case with the spiritual gifts, we don't fully know. That leaves us again in that uncomfortable place of having to discern our experience in light of scripture.

Christy Wilson, the famous missionary to Afghanistan and later professor at Gordon-Conwell seminary recorded in his book, More To Be Desired Than Gold, an interesting story from California many years ago:

Another Afghan Christian I knew, a student, attended a church service while he was visiting in California. During that service the pastor gave a message in tongues. After the service the Afghan went up to speak to the pastor.

"When were you in Afghanistan?" he asked?
"I've never been out of the United States, the pastor replied. "What do you mean?"

"You were talking in Pashtu, my mother tongue," said the Afghan. "You told how Jesus died for my sins and how He rose again from the dead."

"That was the Holy Spirit speaking to you through me," said the pastor. "I have never been to Afghanistan."

The Afghan student recognized this as a miracle. As a result, he has accepted the Lord.[1]

This is a stunning story of how God still uses the gift of tongues in exactly the same way He did on the day of Pentecost. Unfortunately, I have heard very few stories like this.

PRIVATE

The other kind of tongues listed in the Bible, which is the kind that most Pentecostals and Charismatics today operate in, is "praying in tongues."

[14]For if I pray in a tongue, my spirit prays, but my mind is unfruitful. [15]So what shall I do? I will pray with my spirit, but I will also pray with my understanding; I will sing with my spirit, but I will also sing with my understanding. [16]Otherwise when you are praising God in the Spirit, how can someone else, who is now put in the position of an inquirer, say "Amen" to your thanksgiving, since they do not know what you are saying? [17]You are giving thanks well enough, but no one else is edified.

[18]I thank God that I speak in tongues more than all of you. [19]But in the church I would rather

speak five intelligible words to instruct others than ten thousand words in a tongue.

1 Corinthians 14:14-19

A PLACE FOR TONGUES

Here, Paul tells us that tongues are not only for public display, but for private prayer. He encourages others to pray in tongues rather than speak them forth publicly because they build us up personally, but not necessarily others, unless there is interpretation like in the case above about the English pastor. He then goes on to make a bold statement, that He actually prays in tongues more than anyone in Corinth! He makes the distinction of praying in tongues versus speaking them publicly by limiting tongues in a service but fully acknowledges their place in our private prayer life. If Paul prayed in tongues that much, wouldn't that be a good thing for us to emulate today?

So, with a definition of two types of tongues under our belt, let's answer the question of whether or not tongues are required as evidence of Holy Spirit baptism.

The short answer? No. That is an extra-biblical concept. There is nowhere in scripture that requires tongues as evidence of Spirit baptism. It is, however, a very good evidence of baptism, but not a requirement.

IF THIS THEN THAT?

Just because something is good evidence of something, we cannot make the leap to say that that thing is a required evidence. In most cases of baptism in the Holy Spirit in Acts we are led to understand that the recipients prayed in tongues, but not in every case.

1While Apollos was at Corinth, Paul took the road through the interior and arrived at Ephesus. There he found some disciples 2and asked them, "Did you receive the Holy Spirit when you believed?"

They answered, "No, we have not even heard that there is a Holy Spirit."

3So Paul asked, "Then what baptism did you receive?"

"John's baptism," they replied.

> *4Paul said, "John's baptism was a baptism of repentance. He told the people to believe in the one coming after him, that is, in Jesus." 5On hearing this, they were baptized in the name of the Lord Jesus. 6When Paul placed his hands on them, the Holy Spirit came on them, and they spoke in tongues and prophesied. 7There were about twelve men in all.*

> *Acts 19:1-7*

Here we see just how important the Baptism of the Holy Spirit was to Paul. We also see that it was, in fact, a separate encounter from salvation. But the important thing we see here is that the recipients of the Holy Spirit here spoke in tongues AND prophesied.

That makes it difficult to say with any certainty that one must speak in tongues to be baptized in the Holy Spirit.

ONE EVENT OR TWO?

Another issue we have is whether or not Holy Spirit baptism is a separate encounter from salvation. As I have said, it is very clear biblically that it is. The 120 disciples experienced this as well as new converts in Acts 10:44-47 and in the passage we just read.

But I think a more appropriate question is whether or not people have the Holy Spirit living in them at the point of salvation. That may seem like semantics, but I assure you it is not.

> *16And I will ask the Father, and he will give you another advocate to help you and be with you forever— 17the Spirit of truth. The world cannot accept him, because it neither sees him nor knows him. But you know him, for he lives with you and will be in you.*

> *John 14:16-17*

Jesus promised those of us who are saved that the Holy Spirit would live inside of us. So to me, the appropriate question is not whether Holy Spirit baptism is a separate event from salvation, but whether Holy

49

Spirit indwelling is a separate event. According to John 14, it is not.

Being baptized, or "filled" with the Holy Spirit, seems undeniably a separate encounter from salvation. And I believe there is good evidence in scripture that it was an encounter not that unfamiliar from Old Testament saints.

> [18]When David had fled and made his escape, he went to Samuel at Ramah and told him all that Saul had done to him. Then he and Samuel went to Naioth and stayed there. [19]Word came to Saul: "David is in Naioth at Ramah"; [20]so he sent men to capture him. But when they saw a group of prophets prophesying, with Samuel standing there as their leader, the Spirit of God came on Saul's men, and they also prophesied. [21]Saul was told about it, and he sent more men, and they prophesied too. Saul sent men a third time, and they also prophesied. [22]Finally, he himself left for Ramah and went to the great cistern at Seku. And he asked, "Where are Samuel and David?"
>
> "Over in Naioth at Ramah," they said.
>
> [23]So Saul went to Naioth at Ramah. But the Spirit of God came even on him, and he walked along prophesying until he came to Naioth. [24]He stripped off his garments, and he too prophesied in Samuel's presence. He lay naked

all that day and all that night. This is why peo-
ple say, "Is Saul also among the prophets?"

1 Samuel 19:18-24

BEING FILLED

This is an interesting story about "Holy Spirit baptism," long before most Christians think it existed.
Scripture here clearly claims that it was the Holy Spirit
who fell on Saul and his men, and it looked much the
same as it did in Acts. We also see that in Acts 4:31,
the same believers who had already been baptized in
the Holy Spirit were again filled with the Holy Spirit.
"After they prayed, the place where they were meeting
was shaken. And they were all filled with the Holy
Spirit and spoke the word of God boldly."

I think we as believers would do well to understand
that the Holy Spirit lives inside of us because Jesus
promised that to us. At the point of salvation we
should be baptized in the Holy Spirit, not as a one-
time event, but as the beginning of an ongoing lifestyle.

MAKING ROOM FOR THE HOLY SPIRIT

I will conclude with one last encouraging story. A
friend of mine was attending a Lutheran church in the
1970's. This friend received the baptism in the Holy
Spirit and began speaking in tongues, so he went to

his pastor to share the news with him. The pastor was amazed because he said he had just been reading a diary of Martin Luther where he said he prayed in tongues every day. Up to that point, somehow the pastor had never even heard of people praying in tongues. He was about to lead the final session of the confirmation class many of the youth in the church were going through and my friend encouraged him to add a little tagline to the end of their confirmation prayer. When they were done, he said he would have the children say, "and fill me with the Holy Spirit."

When the pastor had them pray their dedication to Jesus, he added that phrase, and when the students said that, 12 of the 24 children immediately threw their hands in the air and started speaking in tongues. They had never received teaching on tongues, nor had they ever witnessed someone who spoke in tongues before. Their experience was not an environmentally learned phenomenon, but a genuine work of the Holy Spirit operating today just like He did with the early church.

And He still will with you today, if you seek Him.

[1]Wilson, J. Christy, Jr. (1992). More To Be Desired Than Gold. South Hamilton, MA: Gordon-Conwell Seminary.

8

PROPHECY: THE GREATEST SPIRITUAL GIFT

With great power comes great responsibility.

I think some great people besides Spiderman's uncle have said similar things, but it is still very true. We often look to men like Hitler as evil on the highest order, but the truth is that men like Hitler were no more evil than any other evil man. No, men like Hitler only had much greater power and authority to exercise their evil.

POWER AND RESPONSIBILITY

Prophecy carries great power with it. Paul instructed us in 1 Corinthians 14:1 very clearly that we should "eagerly desire gifts of the Spirit, especially prophecy." After making it plain that we must do all things in love or else we do them in vain, Paul encourages us to seek God for the most powerful spiritual gift He gives.

There is no more powerful spiritual gift than prophecy. Imagine why. Healings and miracles tend to draw crowds, as we clearly see in Jesus' ministry, but if even Jesus was not able to convert those who witnessed miracles (thousands at a time in many cases) into followers, we should be wary to think that we will fare much better.

Prophecy, on the other hand, exposes the innermost thoughts and realities of a person. When someone tells you what you prayed in silent and then gives you the answer from the Lord, you can only stand in awe of the God who created the infinite universe taking interest in your little life. This is, by the way, how I feel every time it has happened to me. I am moved to tears writing this as I think of all the times God has graciously spoken to this wretched sinner. I am the prodigal son, undeserving of even being called a servant, but my loving Father has received me as a son and offers me every good thing at His disposal.

Paul said it like this:

> *22Tongues, then, are a sign, not for believers but for unbelievers; prophecy, however, is not for unbelievers but for believers. 23So if the whole church comes together and everyone speaks in tongues, and inquirers or unbelievers come in, will they not say that you are out of your mind?*

24But if an unbeliever or an inquirer comes in while everyone is prophesying, they are convicted of sin and are brought under judgment by all, 25as the secrets of their hearts are laid bare. So they will fall down and worship God, exclaiming, "God is really among you!"

1 Corinthians 14:22-25

GIVING GOD A SEAT AT THE TABLE

Seeking prophecy is the act of giving God a seat at the table of your life. I have personally been the benefactor on many occasions of God confirming or rejecting a decision I have made, as well for the churches I have been involved with. He has kept me and at times those with me on the "narrow path" by His prophetic revelation. Nothing is more helpful in the life of the church than that. Knowing for sure that you're on the right track or knowing for sure you've made the wrong decision is equally as empowering.

That doesn't mean we wait around for God to speak before we do anything. No, we have to continually operate using the wisdom and judgment God has given us, but the prophetic leading of God is indispensable in the life of the church. In my experience, God directs about 10% of the time while He confirms (either positively or negatively) 90% of the time. He wants us to walk in faith, and if our heart is submissive to His and we are asking Him to speak, He will keep us on the right path.

THE PRICE YOU PAY

The church that seeks prophecy is a truly blessed place, indeed, but that blessing does not come without cost. Because prophecy is so powerful, it is rife with abuse. Charlatans and even well-intentioned people can use and abuse it to control and manipulate people. I have seen on too many occasions to count people paralyzed by fear of crossing wrong someone they think is a prophet. I have seen people intimidated to question something someone who they esteem a prophet said. I have seen people hurt and bruised by people who told them some great thing that didn't come to pass because it was spoken not from the Lord, but from a place of presumption or wound.

Prophecy is a powerful, but messy thing. Many believe that Paul issues the warnings in 1 Corinthians 14 because tongues and prophecy are divisive and dangerous and we should steer clear of them and their error. But Paul's warnings are for just the opposite reason. Tongues and prophecy, especially, are so powerful that they need to be handled with care and caution.

ORDER IN A SERVICE

Why would Paul command a church not to allow more than three prophets to speak? If God is speaking, why not let Him speak as much and often as He wants? It is because Paul was very aware of the tendency within human nature to start running away with a good thing. I have been in many a meeting where Paul's rules were not followed. I can personally attest that not much good happens after the second or third prophetic word given in any context.

But seeking prophecy is worth the mess. Proverbs 14:4 says "Where there are no oxen, the manger is empty, but from the strength of an ox come abundant harvests," meaning that without prophecy we have little mess, but we also have little gain. Solomon understood that "poop happens," but that it was also a part of the great gain you receive from those things that poop. If your church decides to start seeking prophecy above all other gifts, you will have lots of "poop," but it will be worth it.

One of the reasons that many churches burn out of the mess that comes along with prophecy is because it is inappropriately pastored. Pastors, you must be very confident in your calling, or you will back down in the hour when your church needs you. If you do not exercise the level of authority and discernment that Paul requires in 1 Corinthians 14:26-33, you will cause harm to your congregation when God wants to bring good.

INTIMIDATION AND DISCERNMENT

We must not be willing to simply accept a "prophet's" words at face value, but we must discern them out. We must be willing to reject them if we feel they are not from the Lord. I have seen many churches, in essence, say "how high" because someone they esteemed a prophet said "jump." Sometimes God even allows us to be tested with bad prophecies to see whether we are committed to discerning what is truly Him or not.

Many years ago, the Lord spoke to me nine times that He was calling me away from ministry into a season of obscurity and rest for four years. I consider two confirming words from the Lord incredibly powerful, so needless to say I have only had the Lord say the same thing to me nine times on one occasion. At the time I did not fully understand that meant I really needed to know on the front end because of how hard the time would be, but that is a story for another day.

After I had fully submitted to what I knew the Lord had spoken to me, I was at a church service where the key apostolic leader of a large group of godly churches called me out and told me that God said I was to begin an increase in ministry and speaking opportunities immediately. The man had the credentials and the track record of being right on these kinds of things, but I knew beyond a shadow of a doubt he was wrong. And I was almost sure the Lord told him to say it to me, as well. I believe the Lord was testing my resolve to rest in Him and lay down the small but rapidly growing ministry He had given to me.

EARNESTLY SEEK PROPHECY

I have written extensively about stories of God speaking prophetically to me on my personal blog. I love to tell of the Lord's goodness in this way, and I encourage you to "earnestly desire spiritual gifts, but especially that you may prophesy." It has the potential for harm, but it has infinitely more potential for good.

Because the One who speaks prophetic words is Good.

9

HEALING, SIGNS AND WONDERS: THE POWER OF GOD AMONG US

I have written extensively on the topic of spiritual gifts, partly because I love the topic and partly because it has been something I've felt the leading of the Lord to do. I believe the supernatural ministry of the Holy Spirit is a vital part of our life and work in the gospel. They are, however, not the gospel.

Spiritual gifts will never supplant the good news about Jesus' birth, life, death, burial and resurrection to redeem us, His fallen creation, to God. Nothing in all eternity will ever surpass the overwhelming greatness of that eternal mystery. Spiritual gifts are not even a close second to God's great news of His salvation for us.

EVANGELISM

Spiritual gifts are, however, part of His plan to spread the good news. I have already mentioned before the church's prayer in Acts 4:28-30. It is a crucial part of the story of the church. Let's read it again.

> *29Now, Lord, consider their threats and enable your servants to speak your word with great boldness. 30Stretch out your hand to heal and perform signs and wonders through the name of your holy servant Jesus."*
>
> *31After they prayed, the place where they were meeting was shaken. And they were all filled with the Holy Spirit and spoke the word of God boldly.*
>
> *Acts 4:28-31*

It is important to understand why the church asked God for healings, signs and wonders. They weren't concerned with having cool stories to tell. They didn't ask for supernatural power to increase their wealth or visibility in their community. They didn't ask so they could start on a conference speaking tour. They asked for healings, signs and wonders to increase their boldness to share the gospel.

BOLDNESS

They had just been thrown in prison for boldly declaring the good news about Jesus because a crowd had gathered when they healed a man. They knew that if God would back up their preaching with healings, signs (a prophetic term) and wonders (a generic term for God doing super-cool supernatural stuff), it would increase their boldness like it had before. To make a point that God liked that prayer, He shook the place where they were. What did it do? It further increased their boldness!

It didn't increase their boldness for just anything. It increased their boldness for the gospel, and that is they key we must focus everything on. If we want God to pour out supernatural ministry in our lives, we have to get very serious about the gospel. We must study it. We must understand it. We must live it. We must breath it. We must proclaim it.

I knew a seminary professor who said that only about 10% of his upper-level students could explain the gospel. Seminary students!

God still loves to attest and approve of His message, the gospel, by backing up our words with healings, signs and wonders just like He did for the apostles and early disciples. Don't misunderstand this: God is not approving of us when He pours out His miraculous power. He is approving of the message we bear of Him. If it were the messenger God was approving of, we can point to just as many bad actors in scripture as we have today.

FOR HIS GLORY

Think about Peter. He had regressed back into disassociating with Gentiles and teaching circumcision (Galatians 2:11-13), then going on to preside over the church in Rome. That is horrendously scandalous! If you were to put Peter's life into perspective today, it would be like someone recanting of a tremendous heresy and still later becoming the leader of the church in the largest city in the world with God pouring out miracles. God definitely loved Peter, John, Paul and the rest of the disciples and apostles, but He didn't pour out His supernatural power because of them, but for the sake of the gospel.

Do you want God to pour out healings, signs and wonders when you pray and preach? Preach the gospel! Ask God to speak. Ask God to heal. Ask God to work miracles. I have met far too many people who want God to give them a prophetic word and direct them on what to do next with no thought of the gospel or obeying those words. Often I've seen people do that with money, prestige and honor in mind. James had bad things to say about that:

> *You do not have because you do not ask God.*
> *³When you ask, you do not receive, because you*
> *ask with wrong motives, that you may spend*
> *what you get on your pleasures.*
>
> *James 4:2b-3*

Ask, Seek, Knock

Asking the Lord for healings, signs and wonders to increase your "stuff" is a losing proposition. Don't do it. Just don't. If you want to supercharge your supernatural experience with God, make your life about two things: loving God with all your heart, soul, mind and strength, and loving others like you love yourself.

I encourage you to follow the apostles' early example. Ask God first to give you boldness to share the gospel, and then at the same time ask Him to give you that boldness by backing up your message with healings, signs and wonders.

He may not do it right away, but I guarantee you that if you stick with it, He will give you not only the supernatural encounters you long for, but also a heart so tenderized by the gospel that you will be helpless but to share it with everyone you can.

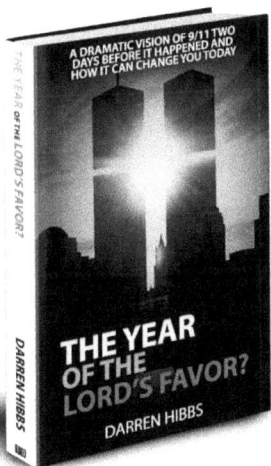

A Sample Chapter from

THE YEAR
OF THE
LORD'S FAVOR?

CHAPTER 1
SEPTEMBER 11, 2001

September 11, 2001

I had never had visions like these before. In fact, after these I was not sure if I had ever really had a vision before. What I thought were visions did not look like this. They were not this real and vivid.

These were gripping, eerie, and somewhat menacing. People were on fire, wrapped up like mummies or screaming out pleading for help. I could see their mouths through the bandages crying out or their faces in anguish, but I heard nothing.

Maybe that is what made them so chilling. I only saw the vision, but I did not hear them. The images are forever stained in my mind. I could not figure out what they meant. For two weeks I pondered why I was having these visions of people burning and in pain, and why was I having them on Saturday nights?

But I am getting ahead of myself.

KNOWING GOD HEARS

I grew up being taught that God does not speak anymore, but that all changed in 1995 when I met a prophet for the first time. I was not prophesied over, but the encounter started me questioning whether or not God did still speak. I decided that if He was still speaking, I wanted Him to speak to me, so I began asking.

I asked the Lord for over five years before I ever heard Him speak the first time. That first time was just a year before 9/11 when I had come back from a mission trip in Guatemala during the summer of 2000. It was a family friend, Loretta, who was going to be the one to prove to me that God really knew me and heard me.

One night in the mountains of northern Guatemala, I was sleeping on the floor of a pastor's house. His house was big; it had two rooms. The walls were made of hand-sawn lumber straight from the trees that had just been cut down. It ventilated well because there were up to two-inch gaps between the wall boards in places. The eves were open to the outside and there was no ceiling, but it kept most of the rain out. The roof was aluminum, so every drop of the torrential downpour we were in was magnified.

I was in a "mummy" backpacking sleeping bag trying to keep the gnats that seemed to be pouring into our bedroom from biting me. I had never met a gnat that bit before, but these guys seemed to like the way I

69

tasted. I sealed myself inside the sleeping bag so that very little air was getting out and my breath was heating the inside to an uncomfortable temperature.

It was around 50 degrees outside, but I was sweltering inside my bag. I passed the time by trying to squish the gnats that were biting me. After what seemed like ten hours, I heard one of my companions I was sharing the dirt floor with stir.

"What time is it?" I asked.

"11:30," he responded.

"It's only been an hour since I went to bed!" I thought to myself.

I was in misery. I could not take this anymore. The gnats were terrible. It felt like thousands of them were biting me simultaneously at all times. I cried out to God:

"God, You've got to do something about these gnats! This is the worst night of my life!"

It was not the most spiritual of prayers, but it was definitely one of the most genuine in my life. About two minutes later one of my companions shouted, "I can't take it anymore!" and ran out of the room into the pastor's bedroom. We heard mumbling in the room next door and very shortly afterward Craig emerged with a coffee can filled with a smoking corn cob. We were all confused because the pastor did not speak Spanish and we did not speak his language.

"Craig, do you speak Ixil?" I asked him.

"Apparently," he smugly responded.

That was their solution. The only thing that hates the smoke of a burning corn cob more than people are biting gnats. The smoke was suffocating, but there were about two inches of fresh air right next to the dirt floor. That was enough. The gnats were gone and I was thrilled. I said a little prayer thanking the Lord and went right back to sleep.

A few weeks later I returned to Texas, and my parents and I sat down with Loretta. She started in with this story.

"I had a dream one night where you were being attacked by thousands of little demons and you were sweating profusely! The demons looked like little bugs. Your mother told me it was cold in the mountains where you were going but I saw you sweating. I heard you pray and ask for help."

I had not said a word to anyone about that story. Loretta could have only known that if God had shown her. She showed me the time she woke up and it just so happened to be 11:30pm, exactly when I had asked what time it was.

Six times Loretta read to me from her journal and each time she told me what happened on those six different occasions where I had cried out to God. He heard me each time, and spoke to someone else on my behalf in precise detail.

CHANGED FOREVER

That was a life-changing experience to know that God heard me, knew me, and saw me. He cared enough about me to speak to me prophetically through another person and tell me He heard everything I asked.

After Guatemala I was energized to seek the Lord even more to hear His voice. I was forever ruined to live without it once I knew He would actually speak to me. Over the next twelve months, He did not let me down.

One night I had a dream where I got a "0" on a test from a professor because he said I cheated. I woke up in a cold sweat because the end result of the dream was that I was kicked out of school because I got so mad at the accusation that I had cheated.

By the next morning when I went to that class, I had already forgotten about the dream. My professor came around at the beginning of class handing out tests, but when he slapped mine on the desk it had a big red "0" at the top.

I immediately looked at him and asked, "Why did you give me a zero?"

"Because you cheated," was his curt response; then he moved on to the next desk.

It was not until I was about to tell him what I thought of him that I remembered the dream. It took my breath away, literally. I could not speak when I thought about how God had warned me not to respond out of anger to something only He knew was about to happen within a few hours of my dream.

Over the course of a few weeks I was able to convince my professor that I had not cheated, but I was stunned that the Lord cared enough about me to keep me from getting angry at the professor. Instead, I was calm and won him over by gently asking him to reconsider, assuring him I had not cheated. In the end, he gave me a "100" on the test. I feel like it was God's way of showing me I had passed His test.

CLOSER TO HOME

Later that year I spent the summer of 2001 in Japan as a short-term missionary, and I had a wonderful time enjoying the beauty of Japan and the warm and hospitable people I met there. It was an enjoyable time of productive ministry where I built many beautiful relationships.

While there I had my third experience where God clearly spoke to me. I had a dream about my brother getting cut across his nose by a guy trying to stab him in the eye. In my dream he pulled his head back just in time and got a gash straight across his nose. People descended around him as the dream ended, and when I woke up, I cried out to God for an hour to spare my brother's life. When I got back to the U.S. a few weeks later, I went to visit him; he had a cut straight across his nose. He told me the story, and it was exactly like my dream. The Lord sent people quickly to protect him from his assailant since the blood from his nose blinded him.

I knew that the Lord involved me in what was going on with my brother, Richard, so I could partner with God in prayer. He wanted me to know what was happening and be part of the solution. God offered me the chance to partake in supernaturally saving my brother's life. God wanted my intercession at the moment of my brother's need.

When I pondered all this, it filled me with an unusual sense of excitement and anticipation. I was a senior in college now, so much of the anxiety that plagues a student was gone, and I was in a place where I was seeking God more and feeling His tangible presence more than I had ever felt before. That led me to start a new routine before going to bed.

I wanted to be more intentional about seeking God, especially in dreams, so I decided that I would incorporate a short little prayer into my bedtime routine.

"Lord, here I am. Speak to me."

It was just a short little prayer, but I wanted to go to bed with the Lord on my mind and willingly offer myself as a conduit for Him to speak. I knew I could not make God speak, but I was sure that the more I asked the more He would!

AUGUST 25, 2001

I did not do very well the first few weeks of trying out my bedtime routine. One of the hardest parts of asking God to speak is just remembering to do it. It does not take fancy words, just words. I probably only remembered to pray a few times that first week, but I did remember to pray on Saturday night.

I spent the evening of Saturday, August 25th, 2001, with some friends and had a great time. I came back to my apartment and spent some good time in prayer and reading God's Word. I went to bed with a feeling of God's great love over me, and I remembered to say my little bedtime prayer.

I got cozy under my covers, and just before I laid down I prayed, "Lord, here I am. Speak to me." Then I quickly laid my head down and closed my eyes.

I was not prepared for God taking my prayer so literally, so fast. That first vision started immediately. I saw people's faces streaming past me from right to left. As a person got closer to the center of my field of vision, they were magnified so I only saw their face. Each different person was in such great anguish from the flames that were in the background of my vision that their cries to me distorted their faces. These tortured souls cried out to me for help, but I heard nothing.

I was gripped for about 45 seconds to a minute before the vision ended as abruptly as it had begun. I was so shocked and perplexed by what I saw I sat up again. I have to admit that I was a little scared.

What did it mean? What was I supposed to do? I knew I was supposed to pray and ask God to show me the meaning, but I had no idea where to start. I was still so new to all this that I was confused as to how I was even supposed to begin. All the experiences I had hearing God up to now were so literal, and this seemed so mysterious.

I prayed for a while, but I eventually went back to bed after hearing nothing further from the Lord. One thing I was sure of was that I had heard from God. What I did not know was what I was supposed to do with it.

The next morning all I could think about was my vision. I pondered and prayed and pondered and prayed. At church I told the pastor, "I feel like people may feel like their world is burning. Maybe we can pray for them after the service." He agreed. He invited some people up afterward and we prayed for them.

I wish that instead of trying to interpret something I did not understand to make it fit my situation, I had just told the pastor what had happened. I did not know back then that is what I should have done. It might not have changed anything, but I could have at least had help understanding it all.

SEPTEMBER 1, 2001

The next week I struggled again to make my new bed-time routine truly routine. A funny thing happened, though. That next Saturday night was almost exactly like the previous. I went to bed after having a great time with friends and after having a good bit of time in prayer and the Word that evening.

Remembering my experience from the previous week, I said my little prayer, laid my head down and closed my eyes. Immediately another vision appeared.

There was one person, wrapped up like a mummy, screaming from behind the bandages. Again there was fire behind him, and he was in utter torment. Was this hell? Was I seeing someone in trouble? My mind raced as the vision persisted. The person struggled to get loose from their mummy bandages but could not.

Again, it lasted about 45 seconds to a minute and then ended as quickly as it had started.

I sat up in shock. This week I was really vexed. "What is going on?" I wondered. I prayed and prayed and pleaded with God to give me an answer. He spoke nothing, so I went back to bed.

The next morning I again pleaded with God for some clarity but I got nothing. Just like the previous Sunday, I told the pastor some strange line like, "I feel like people feel trapped. Maybe we should pray for them today." We had a prayer time at the end and prayed for people who felt trapped in their lives.

I look back on my attempts to understand a super-natural encounter without God's input as just silly. It makes me laugh and groan all at the same time.

SEPTEMBER 8, 2001

I made sure the following week that my Saturday eve-ning routine stayed the same. I was not sure what to do with it, but I knew I had a formula for hearing from God so I was going to stick to it. I figured if I just kept hearing from God, eventually it would make sense.

That night I prayed my prayer, laid my head down on my pillow and closed my eyes with full anticipation of another vision starting immediately.

Nothing. I waited ten seconds and still no vision. Maybe God just needed a little more time.

I sat back up. I grinned as an idea flashed through my head. "I'll give God another chance," I thought. "It can't hurt!"

"Lord, here I am. Speak to me," I said. I quickly laid back down and closed my eyes. Again there was nothing. I waited for a minute with no vision and I finally gave up. I knew it was up to God to give a vision, but if He did not want to He did not have to. I knew I had not imagined them the two weeks before, and I was not going to force myself to conjure one up. I told the Lord "thank you" for the previous two weeks and quickly fell asleep.

But instead of a vision, I had a dream that night. In it, I was walking around lower Manhattan with an angel. I had never been to New York before and I had certainly never seen an angel, in real life or in a dream. In the dream I was excited to be in New York because I had always wanted to visit there. When I am excited about something new, I get very chatty. Apparently this is also true about me in dreams.

I went on and on as I told the angel what all the buildings were (I had studied them in college) and how excited I was to be there. It was as if he and I had been friends for a long time. I knew in the dream he was an angel, but I still treated him as a friend. I was not afraid of him so I used him as a sounding board. At one point I could have sworn I caught him rolling his eyes at me!

Other than his possible exasperation with me he was completely intense. He was unwaveringly focused on something, but I never stopped talking to ask what or why. He would not look at me or speak, he did not respond to anything I was saying and he led me around the city until we came to a particular place.

We abruptly stopped when we reached the place where he was leading me, and just as ominously as he had been walking, he stopped, turned and looked directly in front of him. I had not ever stopped chatting away about all the cool places I wanted to go see there until he stopped. His solemn face gazing into the distance finally put a stop to my relentless jabbering.

I had yet to turn and see what he was looking at. I looked into the angel's eyes as he gazed past me. He was so fixated on something, and it almost looked to cause him pain. I have never seen eyes like that since. They were not heavenly or otherworldly; they looked very human, but they were tortured by what was to come next.

SHEER TERROR

I finally turned and looked to see the World Trade Center's twin towers. I immediately lost my sense of sobriety of the moment and began chatting again about how I had always wanted to visit New York just to go to the observation deck of the World Trade Center. I jabbered away about how tall they were, how they were built and how much I admired them. The angel paid no attention to me whatsoever and again I closed my mouth as I realized my guide was in terrible pain over something.

Not long after I became quiet the angel held out his hand, open palmed, to point at the World Trade Center. I looked down his arm past his hand toward the twin towers, and as soon as I laid my eyes on them they collapsed straight into the ground. I was puzzled why they had sunk straight down instead of falling over, but before I had too much time to ponder that, thousands of people started streaming past us.

Their faces were filled with horror, shock and terror. They came running at us quickly and before too long they were streaming past us by the thousands. Each one looked as if they were running for their lives.

As they streamed past us, I stood there unfazed and unaffected by what had just happened. I was so unaffected that I looked at my angelic guide and uttered words I have never stopped hearing ring through my ears since.

> *"Well, that sucks! Now I'll never get to go up and visit the observation decks of those buildings!"*

Again I could have sworn he rolled his eyes at me and that is when I got it. Finally I realized what had just taken place. My heart had been cold to the human tragedy that was taking place before me because I did not know how to put into context what was happening to me. As soon as I realized the World Trade Center had collapsed and there were possibly lots of people dead, I felt the grave reality that had so gripped the angel.

Shortly after I had gotten the point of what the angel was trying to show me, the dream changed. The buildings were gone, the people were back to normal and the place where they had been was leveled. The angel again held out his hand, open palmed, to point to what was coming.

I saw a small, white building grow up in the place of the twin towers. It looked about three to four stories high and on top I saw what looked like an amphitheater. People started gathering on top of the building and a band got on the small stage there. They began a worship concert and my heart was filled with tremendous hope.

There were 300 to 400 people on top of that building worshipping God, but the meeting ended quickly and I was disappointed. In the dream I knew that the people on top of that building were a small, holy group of people who had turned their hearts to worship God after the tragedy, but I was saddened that it was so short-lived and so small. Given the size of New York and the immensity of the tragedy, I expected so much more.

I immediately woke up feeling the sadness of the short-lived worship movement. I sat awake for quite some time pondering what had just happened. I had never seen an angel in a dream before and as of this writing I have not since. The whole dream was by far one of the most vivid and distinct things that has ever happened to me, awake or asleep.

I eventually went back to sleep, but when I woke up again it was all I could think about. I was asking God what it meant, and just like the previous two weeks I got nothing. I went to church that Sunday morning and, just like the last two weeks, told the pastor something I now think is so silly.

"I think this morning people feel like their world is falling down," I told him, trying to make something out of what I had experienced the night before. We prayed for several people and went to lunch. I could not possibly imagine God wanted to speak to me about something larger than my little sphere of influence.

I wish I had thought more about what the dream meant or that I had told someone to have them help me figure it out, but I did not. I did not think about the dream again. I left the church and it was not even a passing thought.

Well, not until...

SEPTEMBER 11, 2001

I woke up on Tuesday, September 11th, 2001 a little later than normal. I did not have anything pressing that day; I was a college student after all. My roommates had already gone to class, so I was enjoying a leisurely and quiet breakfast alone in my apartment. We had a 13" TV with rabbit ear antenna that we rarely watched; it sat unused as usual that morning. I ate my breakfast quietly, completely unaware the world had dramatically changed outside my door.

About 8:45 that morning my sister, Stephanie, called me.

"Darren, the World Trade Center just collapsed." Her tone was serious.

Waiting for the inevitable "gotcha" moment, I calmly replied, "Sure it did, sis. Sure it did."

"No, I'm serious. Planes flew into them and both buildings just collapsed."

We are practical jokers around our house, so I was not going to let her pull one over on me too easy, but I was not sure where this one could be going. I did not understand why she would be making a big deal out of this. Where was the joke?

I was not thinking at all about my dream. I have often wondered how the only dream I have ever had with an angel would not have immediately come to mind when she started in like this, but it just did not.

"Turn on the TV, Darren," Stephanie said. I could not remember ever hearing her voice shake like that before.

I turned on the little black and white television, but the picture was always slow to come on. It took a full 30 seconds for that old tube to warm up its pixels, but the timbre of the announcers' voices was all I needed to hear.

I do not remember how I ended the phone conversation with Stephanie. Those first thirty seconds of nothing but audio from my television seemed like an eternity. My dream came flooding back and replayed in my mind a hundred times before I saw my first glimpse of what had happened. Then, as we would all watch twenty times a day for weeks to come, I saw it.

The screen warmed up just in time for a replay of the first tower collapsing straight down into the ground. Then they replayed the second tower as it identically descended into the earth.

"Oh my God," I said as I dropped the phone to my side. "What have you done?" All I could think about was that I had already seen this. And just like that, a dream I had days before became my and everyone else in America's reality.

THE DAY THAT WOULD NOT END

Why had God shown this to me? What was going on here? What did this mean? A thousand questions raced through my mind as time stood still.

I was glued to the television for what seemed like the next ten years. Time stood still for so many Americans that day, but for me, all I could do was sit in silence as I watched the replay of my dream for all the world to see over and over and over again.

I cannot remember much else about that day except that I sat there watching the towers fall over and over again thinking about what I should have done. I thought time and again about how stupid I had been for three weeks. I kept thinking how silly I was to think God was showing me those visions and an angelic dream so we could have a cool Sunday service. All of a sudden I was overcome with guilt that I had not clued in.

"Maybe I could have stopped this," I told myself a hundred times that day. I kept asking myself, "Why did I not tell someone? Why would God have shown this to me if He did not want me to do something about it?"

I endured the rest of the day haunted by my thoughts. Haunted by what could have been. What should have been. I did not sleep that night. I could not tell my roommates what had happened to me. I could not tell anyone. I felt ashamed and embarrassed that I had been so foolish.

MAKING SENSE OF IT ALL

I lived in a fog for weeks after 9/11. I was so overcome by grief and guilt that I did not know how to cope. I spent most evenings alone after that trying to figure out why God had shown me those events three days earlier and why I had not done anything about it.

It came to a head as I found myself aimlessly driving around town one evening several weeks later. I quickly parked my car when I felt the surge of tears come over me. I laid my head into the steering wheel and cried out, "Why God? Why me? Why did you show this to me?"

"Because you're my friend, and I like to tell my friends what I'm thinking about."

As my head lay against the steering wheel, those words resounded through my body. Maybe I had not screwed up. Maybe I was not responsible for those peoples' lives after all. Maybe this whole thing was just God being a friend to me.

It seemed a little far-fetched at that moment, but those words brought instant comfort to my soul. I lifted my head up with a little more confidence. "If God knew these things were going to happen so that He showed me, He is smart enough to know that I was not going to do anything about it," I thought to myself. Maybe He really was just showing me what was on His heart.

I would like to say that I started feeling better about it all right then, but honestly it was months before I could let go of the idea that if I had said something, maybe I could have prevented thousands of people from dying. Honestly, looking back on it I am glad I did not. I am pretty sure now that if I had said something I would be prisoner #1 at Guantanamo Bay.

But nothing took away the question of "why?" Why me? Why that? Why an angel? Why the visions of people burning? God went to great lengths to highlight for me something that was going on in a place thousands of miles away.

As time went on, I could not help but think there must be something more that I was missing. Why would God go to such extraordinary lengths (at least from my perspective) to tell me about the most heinous act of aggression in America during my lifetime?

My answer came in another unexpected way.

This book is available at Amazon.com in paperback, hardcover and for your Kindle eBook reader.

ABOUT THE AUTHOR

Darren Hibbs has worked in industry and in full-time ministry. As a writer, he has published several books.

Darren has great passion for revival in America and longs to see the church embrace God's correction so that we may receive the fullness of what He has to offer us.

Darren's heart burns to bring a message of hope to a lost and broken world through the immeasurable love of Jesus. It is his heart that the church will grow in love for God and embrace His love and power so that the lost will see and hear the good news about Jesus as they see it change us.

Darren writes regularly and can be reached at www.DarrenHibbs.com.

OTHER BOOKS BY DARREN HIBBS

Do you wonder if God still speaks to us today? Do you long to hear from Him? Darren Hibbs grew up believing God no longer spoke, but that changed when God actually started speaking to Him in dreams that literally came true.

These stories will encourage and strengthen your walk with the Lord through real-world experiences of asking for Him to communicate His love, direction and hope. Get ready to read stories that will spur you on to ask the Lord to speak to you too.

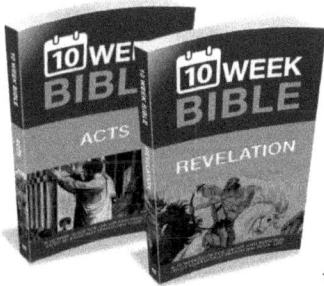

The 10 Week Bible Study is a different kind of Bible Study that will take you deep into the scriptures and cause you to engage God's Word like never before.

With helpful commentary and probing questions, the 10 Week Bible study will help you find a new love for God's Word. Ten weeks really can change your life!

www.ingramcontent.com/pod-product-compliance
Lightning Source LLC
Chambersburg PA
CBHW071818020426
42331CB00007B/1537